MW01506408

The Short Story
of
One Tough Cookie

The Short Story
of
One Tough Cookie

A TRUE STORY

Never Crumble!

♡ Isabella
2019

written and illustrated by
Isabella Sementilli

The Short Story of One Tough Cookie
A True Story
Copyright © 2018 by Isabella Sementilli

All rights reserved. No part of this book may be used or reproduced in any form, electronic or mechanical, including photocopying, recording, or scanning into any information storage and retrieval system, without written permission from the author except in the case of brief quotation embodied in critical articles and reviews.

Illustrated by Isabella Sementilli
Book design by The Troy Book Makers

Printed in the United States of America

The Troy Book Makers • Troy, New York • thetroybookmakers.com

To order additional copies of this title, contact your favorite local bookstore or visit www.shoptbmbooks.com

ISBN: 978-1-61468-467-1

Mom and Dad ~ Thank you for... EVERYTHING!
Santino ~ Even though you beat me at every game–
you're the best brother and friend ever!
Luca ~ Thanks for always sitting with me–
a dog is really a girl's best friend.
Most importantly, I thank God for giving me
the strength to get through each day.

To all those who have suffered from a concussion
and all brain injury survivors– just remember...
we are all tough cookies and we won't crumble!

~ When life gives you lemons, you can make
lemonade – or really yummy cookies. ~ Isabella

My name is Isabella—

Izzy some say.

They are both me and I prefer both I must convey.

I have a short story of an awful, unforgettable day to share.

It's a story of how I got injured when a girl in my class acted very unkind, didn't even care.

It's a story all about me.

I guess we can say it's

a "mini-autobiography."

Be sure to listen with ears open as wide as a whale,

as I now begin my very true tale....

It was October 21, 2013, a beautiful fall morning,

and the leaves were no longer green.

I was excited to start my school day– to learn and play.

Unfortunately for me, it would not be a good day.

I got my chair pulled out from beneath me as I went to sit down.

I went straight to the nurse with jillions of tears and a very big frown.

I held ice on my head and hoped the pain would go away.

I couldn't take the pain anymore and did not want to learn or even play.

My parents were called and they rushed to pick me up.

I jumped into my dad's arms and felt like a newborn pup.

Next, we were off to my doctor for a long check-up.

My day ended with sadness, pain, and chamomile tea in a cup.

The next day was so bad as I tried to get out of bed.

It felt like a boulder just fell on my head.

I yelled for my mom and she came running in.

"No school," she said, and ran to get me some aspirin.

I wanted to scream, yell, shout—

"This can't be! Please mom, I love school no doubt!"

I was now a proud fifth grader. Excited to learn and
do my homework later.

So many new things to learn and fun projects to do.

I have art, gym, chorus, and kickball at recess too!

Wait!! This was the year of the amazing Fifth Grade Talent Show.

It would be my year to shine– to glow.

I had it all planned since third grade just what I would do–

something that I absolutely loved– as much as a cow loves to moo.

I would tap my little feet right across the stage.

It would be the absolute best and my friends would all be so engaged!

So much fun to be had, so much to do.

Please, I beg, please body work with my head!

Please do something to get me out of my bed.

I had pain from my eyes all the way to my tailbone,

and even though I tried to fall asleep— I could not get in that zone.

Bed? Bed? How long can I stay here? This I surely dread!

I missed a whole week of school.

No reading, writing, or seeing my friends.

School was the best.

Sadly, now all I could do was lay in bed and rest.

I was achy and sore.

My body felt awful.

It was November and the weather started getting cool.

Being home was more the norm than being in school.

My eyes had sharp stabbing pains that went into my head,

to the point where it was uncomfortable to even lay in my bed.

I couldn't watch television or use the computer.

No tap dance or tennis.

No riding my scooter.

Oh, what a shame!

Instead, I played with mom and my brother Sonny,
one too many board games.

My whole body ached from morning until night.

My pain was relentless– like an opponent after a knock-out fight.

The pain I had went into my skull and my neck.

My mother said, "We should definitely have that checked."

Many x-rays and MRI scans were to come next,

as we went from doctor to doctor and specialist to specialist.

WOW!

This was a nightmare and so very complex!

I started physical therapy to try to ease some of my pain.

Many back and neck rubs, but it all hurt the same.

My physical therapist was so very sweet,

and that in itself I thought was a very nice treat.

The pain throughout my body was constant and would not go away.

I cried a lot and would constantly pray.

More physical therapy and doctors too,

and still with no physical activity for me—

many more games of Scrabble and Clue.

My pain was constant.

Morning.

Noon.

Night.

This was crazy. This was not right.

The tight-rope squeezing, needle stabbing pain in my head,

was really something awful—

something I totally dread.

I had pain from my tailbone, right up to my light-sensitive eyes—

which would obviously explain all my tears and all my cries.

So this is what happens when you get a concussion,

your brain gets rattled

like a drummer playing percussion.

The light was so blinding and so very bright.

Please shut all the curtains to make it all right!

Please turn off the television– the sound is hurting my ears.

I am flipping and flopping.

How can I eliminate all my new fears?

headache
sensitivity to sound
dizzy   confusion

You see, when my head got rattled, my brain took a blow.

Even though you don't see my actual symptoms— believe me— I know.

Light bothers my eyes.

Sounds around me are like piercing cries.

My head is spinning and although I may be grinning—

my pain is very real.

fatigue   dazed

sensitivity to light

nausea   slurred speech

vomiting

I was exhausted and irritable.

I was very sad too.

Sometimes I snapped at my brother for no reason—

did I belong in a zoo?

Who was I? This wasn't me.

All of this was happening because I suffered a concussion—

also known as a TBI or brain injury.

Everything I loved to do was gone in one instant.

Tap dance, tennis, even running around– all of that was now very distant.

You see– the moment my classmate made a choice to pull out my chair–

was the moment my life turned into a never-ending nightmare!

My head flew back and my neck hit the hard plastic chair–

it wasn't good– it wasn't fair.

I went down hard on the floor.

Not a part of the classroom I would choose to explore.

I went down with a big, loud BAM!

I felt all tingly and weird like I was just hit by a ram.

No recess with my friends.

I couldn't play gym.

No running around or taking a quick swim.

Yikes! I am unable to do a ton!

For an active kid like me,

this surely was no fun!

Sitting around doing nothing was really no fun.

I decided to put on some shades and go out in the sun.

I decided no one could hold me down.

No bully would be able to break my crown.

Here I was back on my feet.

Still no tap or tennis, just something to get me out of my seat.

Time to learn something new.

Perhaps I would build a building or two.

Well maybe someday...

Hmmmmm...

Deep breath.

Stay positive.

I got this. I just need to start slow.

I will not get dragged down and just go with the flow.

I will not let my smile become a permanent frown.

So I thought a bit longer....

Yes! That's it!

I will learn how to knit.

I always did admire a pretty pink snit.

I called my nana's friend and she gave me her kit.

She sat and taught me how to turn a ball of string

into an absolutely, wonderful, beautiful thing!

Now I make scarves for mom, dad, and Sonny too!

Even my dog Luca enjoys them—

if not just for the chew.

Woohoo! I can do it! Happy little me!

Knitting was great fun, but after a while,

mom didn't know what to do with that great big pile.

I felt I needed something else to do...

something totally different, totally new.

I walked and wandered.

Sat and pondered.

Oh, goodness!

What do I do?

I went to see my papa and asked him to help me bake.

Perhaps a bread, a cookie, Stromboli or cake?

He agreed. With smiles on our faces, off to work we went.

I took a few recipes that papa lent

and went home to my kitchen to see what I could change, what I could reinvent.

After a while, I decided cookies would be my thing.

I twerked and tweaked a recipe that papa had showed me.

I stayed in the kitchen from early morning to quarter past three.

Although my head was pounding and I was totally exhausted, this beautiful cookie was finally frosted.

The smell of my cookies filtered all through the house.

Flour covered my apron, right through to my blouse.

My heart was filled with happiness and joy,

like on Christmas morning when Santa brings that one special toy.

I felt like I needed to share my creation with all.

My cookies.

Yes! I will stand tall.

These special cookies were made by me.

I felt so happy and wanted the whole world to see.

Just like you and me, no two cookies were the same.

My cookies– unique and different– now needed a name.

I thought and thought.

My cookies needed to stand out from the crowd.

They needed a name that would make me feel proud.

That's when the name popped into my head—

IZNETTES!

Yes! That's it!

Now off to bed.

Iznettes were born that very day.

My very own creation.

Hip, hip hooray!

My cookies were such a hit!

I was making so many with hardly a minute to sit.

Each cookie I make is made with lots of love.

It makes me so happy—

like a peaceful, pink dove.

Diagnosed with PTSD, a concussion, back and neck injuries too,
some days it hurts so bad, I can't even chew.
I have been on this unfortunate journey for too many years,
which have been accompanied by pain and buckets of tears.

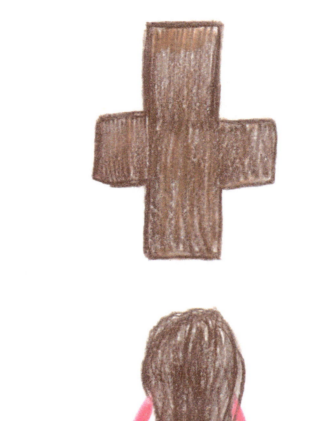

Knowing my smile was always inside—
FAITH
gave me a reason to make it shine— become magnified.
So with a smile on my face, I went about my day—
trying to stay happy and cheerful in my own little way.

Unfortunately, I was met with so many bewildered looks and whispering words of people questioning me...

"Is she really even hurt?"

"She must be okay."

"She is smiling. She looks fine."

Please, make them stop! Why all the dismay?

See there is an awful misconception,

for those who have gotten
an unfortunate concussion.

There is no bump.

No bruise.

No cast.

Nothing visible to the eye.

It hurts so bad and can even
make grown men cry.

This is real what I feel,

so please let me be.

I am in pain, hurting too, even though
your eyes can't see.

I was physically hurt and have lasting internal scars.

Sometimes, emotionally I felt like I belonged on planet Mars.

But look at me now.

I got me to be as fierce as a crocodile.

I am...

STRONG.

I am...

EMPOWERED.

I am bursting with happy emotions and want to be sure,

I can help lift someone's spirits and spread my happiness–

give people the "Izzy Cure"......

Be nice.

Be kind.

Share a smile.

Perhaps I could just help out a person in need–

help them see that being mean

is just plain awful and not part of their genes.

I sat and thought how me, little Izzy—

(who still gets very light-headed and sometimes quite dizzy),

could take my cookie sales and have them go toward something positive, something good.

I knew that would make me feel happy and perhaps understood.

I decided to donate to charities and give back to my neighborhood.

Golden Rule

Do unto others
As you would have others
Do unto you.

I am hopeful that from my short story you will see,

how the unkind actions of another has totally changed me.

Please keep your hands to yourself, right by your side.

Invading someone's space isn't nice, it's not wise.

You see, pulling someone's chair out is dangerous and downright cruel.

Calling people names is not part of the Golden Rule.

Hurting someone is really just not nice, not smart.

It could leave someone with a big, broken heart.

bullying

anger

mean

rude

Come on everyone, let's all do our part.

We need little acts of kindness so our world stays together and doesn't fall apart.

be polite

be kind

be thoughtful

be honest

We all can change— just dig deep down inside.

Be happy and put any anger aside.

It's really not hard,

quite easy to do.

Remember—

to be a tough cookie

it's all up to YOU!

be tolerant

be happy

be respectful

THE END